Welcome to
Israel

Meredith Costain   Paul Collins

CHELSEA HOUSE PUBLISHERS
Philadelphia

This edition first published in 2002 in the United States of America by Chelsea House Publishers, a subsidiary of Haights Cross Communications

Chelsea House Publishers
1974 Sproul Road, Suite 400
Broomall, PA 19008–0914

The Chelsea House world wide web address is www.chelseahouse.com

Library of Congress Cataloging-in-Publication Data Applied for.
ISBN 0-7910-6876-5

First published in 2002 by
Macmillan Education Australia Pty Ltd
627 Chapel Street, South Yarra, Australia, 3141

Copyright © Meredith Costain and Paul Collins 2002

Edited by Miriana Dasovic
Text design by Goanna Graphics (Vic) Pty Ltd
Cover design by Goanna Graphics (Vic) Pty Ltd
Illustration by Vaughan Duck
Map by Stephen Pascoe

Printed in Hong Kong

Acknowledgements

The author and the publisher are grateful to the following for permission to reproduce copyright material:

Cover photograph: Bar mitzvah, Jerusalem, courtesy of Australian Picture Library/Steve Vidler.

Australian Picture Library/Corbis, pp. 14, 30 (2nd row); Australian Picture Library/Jon Hicks, p. 19 (top); Australian Picture Library/J P & E S Bake, pp. 29, 30 (4th row: left); Australian Picture Library/Noeline Kelly, pp. 21 (top), 30 (6th row); Australian Picture Library/Steve Vidler, pp. 9, 12, 18, 22 (both), 23, 28, 30 (1st row, 4th row: middle & right, 5th row); Fred Adler/Kino Studios, pp. 8, 11 (bottom), 24, 25 (bottom), 27 (top); Lonely Planet Images/Eddie Gerald, p. 25 (top); Lonely Planet Images/Lee Foster, p. 13; Lonely Planet Images/Paul Doyle, p. 10; Lonely Planet Images/Paul Hellander, pp. 11 (top), 19 (bottom), 20, 21 (bottom); Lonely Planet Images/Sara-Jane Cleland, pp. 15, 26; Nina Jawitz, pp. 5, 6, 7 (both); Reuters, p. 27 (bottom).

Contents

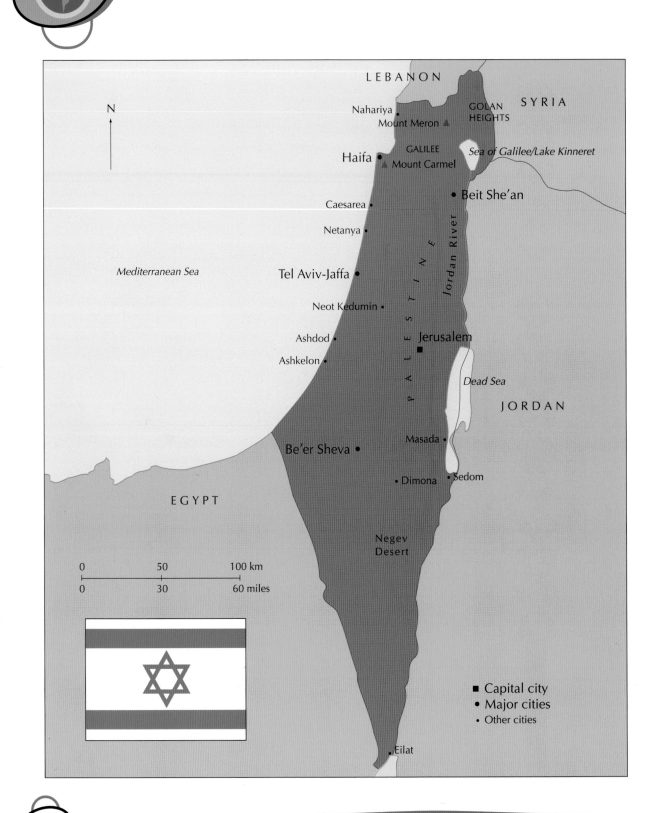

N

LEBANON

SYRIA

Nahariya
Mount Meron ▲

GOLAN
HEIGHTS

GALILEE

Sea of Galilee/Lake Kinneret

Haifa
▲ Mount Carmel

● Beit She'an

Caesarea

Netanya

Jordan River

Mediterranean Sea

Tel Aviv-Jaffa

P
A
L
E
S
T
I
N
E

Neot Kedumin

Ashdod

● Jerusalem

Ashkelon

Dead Sea

JORDAN

Masada

Be'er Sheva ●

● Dimona   ● Sedom

EGYPT

Negev
Desert

0	50	100 km
0	30	60 miles

■ Capital city
● Major cities
• Other cities

• Eilat

Welcome to Israel!

Shalom! My name is Ella. I come from a large city in Israel called Tel Aviv.

Israel is a long, narrow country. It lies along the eastern shore of the Mediterranean Sea, where Europe, Asia and Africa meet. Our neighbors are Lebanon to the north, Syria to the northeast, Jordan to the east, and Egypt to the southwest.

Israel was formed as a country in which Jewish people could live. The region has a long history. Jews lived here thousands of years ago, and this is the land where Christianity first began. The area is also home to many Arab Muslims.

Our flag is based on the design of the Jewish prayer shawl, known as a tallith. It is white and has two blue stripes. In the center is the ancient symbol of the Jews, the Shield of David. Our official emblem is the menorah. This is a seven-branched candlestick used in the synagogue, our place of worship.

Family life

Tel Aviv is a large, busy city on the Mediterranean coast. We live in one of the city's busiest streets. There are **double-glazed** windows in our apartment, and we could not sleep at night without them. Our city has huge rubbish dumps, and the rivers are full of pollution. Tel Aviv is a lovely city – but its noise and pollution make it a difficult place to live. Most of our industries and businesses are based here.

My parents, David and Nina, are both graphic designers. I have a younger brother, Avriel, who is almost seven years old. He is a bit irritating, but I manage to live with him somehow.

*This is my mom and Avriel, playing Snakes and Ladders on our balcony. Our small apartment is in an old building. We **renovated** the apartment and painted every room a different color. I especially like my room because I chose the color myself.*

Last year my family went to visit my grandparents. They live in Zimbabwe. That is my dad standing behind me, in the black T-shirt, with my mom and Uncle Dan.

Lots of Israeli kids like sports, but not me. I am not very good at it. Instead, I like to play on the computer and watch TV. I have a kitten called George. He bites and scratches me all over my hands and feet, but I still love him.

Here I am with one of my paintings. It shows a park in our local area. Two years ago, I had an exhibition at my school. I love painting.

School

Israeli children start school when they are five and must stay at school until they turn 16. Many of us attend pre-school first. After six years of primary school, we spend three years at intermediate school, and another three at secondary school. All Israelis (both young men and women) must then spend up to three years in the **military service**. After that, many go to university or college to train for a career.

My school day starts at 8:15 a.m. and finishes at 3:15 p.m. On Tuesdays and Fridays, we finish at lunchtime. I go to an art school called the Harrison Campus for Arts. I have 11 hours a week of specialist arts studies, where

A group of Israeli children on their way to school.

I study **sculpture**, photography, real-life drawing and painting. I also study French, English, math, history, geography, biology, grammar, society, self-expression, **Zionism**, the Bible, sports and literature. My lessons are all taught in Hebrew. When I finish school, I would like to be a graphic designer, an artist, a writer or a computer programmer.

Sports and leisure

Many Israeli people love sports. Our most popular sports include soccer, basketball, tennis, volleyball and gymnastics. There are organized competitions at local, regional and national levels for many of these sports. Each week, crowds of people turn up at their local stadiums. They cheer enthusiastically for their favorite teams. Israelis also enjoy horse-riding, hang-gliding, fencing and cycling.

The Dead Sea is below sea level. It is the lowest point on earth. The sea is so salty that it is impossible for people to sink, even if they cannot swim!

Our country is small, so most people do not live far from a beach. Popular water sports include swimming, windsurfing, sailing, snorkelling and deep-sea diving. Every year, thousands of Israelis and visitors from other countries take part in the Jerusalem March. This is a 5-kilometer (3-mile) swim across Lake Kinneret (the Sea of Galilee).

Many tourists travel around Israel during their vacations, exploring our many **archaeological** sites. Every four years, Jewish athletes come from all over the world to take part in the Maccabiah Games. The games are known as the 'Jewish Olympics'.

Israeli culture

Israel is a **melting pot** of people from many different countries and cultures. We also remember the traditions of our ancient past. This is often reflected in the art, writing, music and dance of our country's creative artists.

Many authors and poets have written about what it is like to live in Israel. Our great writers include the poet Haim Nahman Bialik, and author Shmuel Yosef Agnon, who won the Nobel Prize for Literature in 1996. Our children's books encourage readers to think and ask questions about the world they live in.

Many Israelis enjoy going to concerts and the theater. Our best-known orchestra is the Israeli Philharmonic Orchestra, which plays over 200 concerts a year. There are large performing-arts complexes in Tel Aviv and Jerusalem. Classical concerts are sometimes performed at the restored Roman **amphitheaters** at Caesarea and Beit She'an. Our six professional dance companies perform both locally and overseas. The Kol-Dmama (Sound and Silence) Dance Ensemble includes dancers who are deaf.

A fiddler plays in the street. When they came to Israel, people brought many of their dances and musical instruments from their 'old countries', such as Romania and Poland.

A modern sculpture on the Promenade in Tel Aviv. There are also many museums around the country which preserve ancient Jewish art.

The early pioneers brought folk dances with them from the cities of Eastern Europe. The most famous dance is the *hora*. It is danced by people linking their arms to form a circle. The *hora* is a symbol of a new way of life in a new land. It is often performed in the streets at festivals such as Independence Day.

Israelis are very keen readers. During Hebrew Book Week, squares and parks in towns and villages around the country become book markets. Every two years, over 1,000 publishers display their latest books at the Jerusalem Book Fair.

Festivals and religion

There are two main Jewish groups living in Israel. One group comes from Central and Eastern Europe. The other group consists of more recent settlers who come from the Islamic countries of North Africa and the Middle East. After World War 2, Jews settled here from many other countries, including Yemen, Ethiopia and the former Soviet Union. There are also over one million non-Jewish citizens living in Israel, mainly Christian or Muslim Arabs. These groups follow their own religious holidays, such as Easter and Ramadan.

Jewish festivals and holidays

The Jewish calendar is based on the phases of the moon, so these dates vary each year.

Rosh Hashanah (Jewish New Year)	September/October
Yom Kippur (Day of Atonement)	October
Sukkot (Feast of the Tabernacles)	October
Hanukkah (Festival of Lights)	December
Purim	March
Passover	April
Remembrance Day	April/May
Independence Day	April/May
Jerusalem Day	May/June

A bar mitzvah ceremony. On their 13th birthdays, Jewish boys have a bar mitzvah, and Jewish girls a bat mitzvah. They will take on the religious duties of an adult from this date.

Every day, Jews gather to pray at the Western Wall in Jerusalem. The wall is all that is left of the Second Temple of Judaism, destroyed by the Romans 2,000 years ago. Known as the Wailing Wall, it is the most sacred (holy) Jewish site in the world.

Most of our public holidays are based on religious festivals. Each group has its own weekly holy day. For Muslims it is Friday, for Jews it is Saturday, and for Christians it is Sunday.

Rosh Hashanah (the Jewish New Year festival) is celebrated in September. We have big feasts at home and go to the synagogue. This is a place where Jewish people pray. The *shofar* (a ram's horn) is blown to mark the end of Yom Kippur – the Day of Atonement. This ends a period called the 'Ten Days of Repentance'. During this time, Jewish people remember the wrongs we have done, and promise to do better next year.

Passover is held each spring. We eat special food such as **matza** on the first night. It reminds us of the time, thousands of years ago, when Jews were released from slavery in Egypt by the **prophet** Moses. For the autumn festival of Sukkot, we set up little shacks outside, made from leaves and branches. These remind us of the tents the Jews lived in after their flight from captivity. Each December, we celebrate Hanukkah, the Festival of Lights. On each day of the festival, we light a candle on a nine-branched candlestick called a *hanukiah.*

Food and shopping

Our people came to Israel from all over the world, so there are many different types of food here. One of the most popular dishes is felafel. These are small fried balls made from chick peas. They are served inside Arab pita bread with pickles, salad and a spicy sauce. There are felafel stalls everywhere. They are the Middle Eastern version of fast food!

Other popular dishes include flaky pastries filled with salty cheese and spinach called *boureka, blintzes* (pancakes stuffed with jam or cheese) and gefillte fish (boiled fish balls). Grapefruit, oranges and avocados are plentiful here. A plaited bread called challah is served for the **Sabbath** meal. During Passover, we eat matza.

Each year, many families prepare a special feast to celebrate Purim. We have a special holiday to remember the time when Queen Esther rescued the Persian Jews.

There are many wonderful markets all over Israel for people to do their shopping. Zalatimo's is a famous sweet shop in the Muslim Quarter of the Old City of Jerusalem. The back room of the shop opens on to the remains of the original entrance to the Church of the Holy Sepulchre.

Most Jewish restaurants, and all public eating places, serve kosher food. This is food that has been prepared according to ancient dietary laws. Strict Jews are not allowed to eat shellfish, or meat from pigs. Meat and dairy foods cannot be prepared together or eaten together.

I usually have cereal for breakfast, and eat my lunch at school. Normally I have potatoes, pasta or sandwiches, followed by homemade cookies. We usually have either a pie or pasta for dinner. This is our main meal of the day, but most people eat lunch as their main meal. My favorite foods are pasta, pies, rice, pizza, couscous, chips, pancakes and sweets.

Make potato latkes

During religious celebrations, Jewish people eat special foods. Donuts and special potato pancakes called *latkes* are eaten at Hanukkah because they are cooked with oil. To us, oil is a symbol of the miracle of the first Hanukkah.

Ask an adult to help you prepare this dish.

This recipe makes about 10 *latkes*.

You will need:

- 2 large potatoes
- 2 eggs, beaten
- 2 tablespoons plain flour
- salt and pepper
- cooking oil
- paper towels

What to do:

1 Peel the potatoes. Grate them into a bowl.

2 Squeeze out any excess juice from the grated potatoes with your hands. Drain the juice from the bowl.

3 Add the eggs, flour, salt and pepper to the grated potatoes.

4 Heat the oil in a frying pan.

5 Drop large spoonfuls of potato mixture into the pan. Flatten them with the back of a spoon.

6 Fry the *latkes* until golden brown on one side. Turn them over and fry the other side.

7 Place the *latkes* on paper towels. Pat them with another towel to absorb extra oil.

8 Serve the *latkes* on small plates.

Grow your own avocado plant

Avocados grow well in our warm climate. They are easy to grow at home too, and make a pretty pot plant. Unfortunately, you will have to wait about seven years before they begin to produce fruit!

You will need:

- a ripe avocado
- a knife
- four wooden toothpicks
- a glass
- lukewarm water
- a plant pot
- potting mix or soil

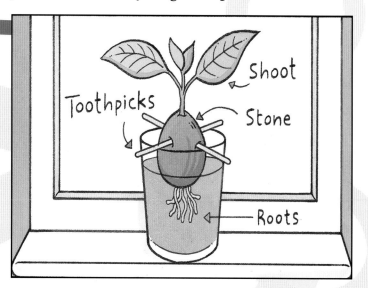

What to do:

1 Remove the stone from the avocado. Scrape away any flesh and wash the stone well.

2 Push the sharp ends of the toothpicks into the stone, around its middle.

3 Fill the glass with lukewarm water. Place the rounded end of the stone into the water, supported by the toothpicks.

4 Put the glass on a windowsill. Choose a spot that is warm and has plenty of light, but receives no direct sunlight.

5 After two months the stone should split, and a thick white root will grow from the bottom. A green shoot will then grow from the top of the stone.

6 When the shoot is about 8 centimeters (3 inches) high, transfer the plant into a pot of soil. Leave part of the stone above the soil. Place the pot in a warm and sunny spot.

Landscape and climate

Israel is long and narrow. It measures 470 kilometers (290 miles) from north to south, and 135 kilometers (84 miles) at its widest point from east to west. Israel is such a small country, you could drive from one end to the other in about nine hours. The landscape you would see on the way, however, is very varied. It includes rugged mountains and hills, inland seas, dry riverbeds, coastal plains and fertile farmland.

A long backbone of mountains runs from north to south. Our highest peak is Mount Meron (1,208 meters (3,960 feet)), in the Galilean highlands of the far north. Lake Kinneret, also known as the Sea of Galilee, is a freshwater lake. It is fed by the Jordan, our longest river. The river eventually flows into the Dead Sea, at the southern end of the Jordan valley.

King Solomon's Pillars are huge redstone pillars in the Timna Valley, north of Eilat. At their base are the ruins of an Egyptian temple.

Israel has many beautiful beaches, including Netanya. Rain only falls along the Mediterranean coast from November to April.

The Golan Heights, in the north of the country, were formed many thousands of years ago by volcanic eruptions. The limestone hills of Galilee are in this area. Galilee is a green and fertile area, with a milder climate and heavier rainfall than the rest of Israel. At the seaside resort of Eilat, there is an underwater national park. Tropical fish can be seen through the clear sea water.

Average temperatures

	January	July
Jerusalem	8°C (46°F)	23°C (73°F)
Tel Aviv	12°C (54°F)	26°C (79°F)
Eilat	15°C (59°F)	33°C (91°F)
Netanya	14°C (57°F)	26°C (79°F)

Both of Israel's major highways run through the Negev Desert. This desert covers 60 percent of Israel. The air shimmers with heat in summer, and it almost never rains here. Some parts of the Negev look like the surface of the moon!

Plants and animals

Many different plants and animals are found in our country. Natural woodlands cover the hilly areas of Galilee and Mount Carmel. In spring, the ground in the north is covered by a carpet of wildflowers. Wild irises, lilies, tulips and hyacinths grow freely here. Date palms and pistachios grow in the Negev Desert.

Over 350 different kinds of birds are found in Israel. Twice a year, hundreds of thousands of birds such as honey buzzards, pelicans and storks stop over on their way to other countries. Mountain gazelles and ibex (a kind of wild goat) roam the hills, while foxes, jungle cats and other mammals live in wooded areas. There are over 80 different kinds of reptiles living here, including chameleons, snakes and agama lizards.

These 2,000-year-old olive trees grow in the Garden of Gethsemane. The garden, in the Old City of Jerusalem, is said to be the place where Jesus was arrested.

There are over 150 national parks caring for endangered animals, such as leopards and vultures. Feeding stations have been set up for wolves, hyenas and foxes. At Neot Kedumin, in the center of the country, a landscape reserve has been set up to collect and look after plants that were mentioned in the Bible. Other wildlife centers raise and care for biblical animals such as ostriches, Persian fallow deer, oryx (antelope), onagers (wild asses) and Somali wild asses. They are then set free.

Avocados grow easily in our mild Mediterranean climate.

Wild ibex can be found in the Negev Desert.

Cities and landmarks

Jerusalem, our capital city, has a long history. Nearly 3,000 years ago, it was the country's capital under King David. His son, King Solomon, built the first Jewish temple in the city. Jerusalem's massive walls contain a mixture of ancient buildings, religious sites and bustling markets. It has importance for three of the world's great religions – Judaism, Christianity and Islam.

The modern city of Tel Aviv was Israel's first new town. It is the center for entertainment and the arts, as well as business and industry. More people live in and around Tel Aviv than in any other part of the country.

The Old City of Jerusalem is surrounded by an ancient wall, and features the beautiful golden Dome of the Rock.

The walls of the Old City were built by the Ottoman Turks in the 1600s. Until 1860, the Old City was divided into Armenian, Christian, Jewish and Muslim quarters. It contains landmarks such as the Western Wall, which is part of the temple built by King Herod. Also in the Old City is the golden Dome of the Rock, a Muslim shrine. Muslims believe that the prophet Mohammed ascended to Heaven from here to talk to God.

The New City has grown up over the past 100 years. It contains modern buildings such as shopping centers, office blocks and the Knesset – Israel's parliament.

Around 2,000 years ago, King Herod built a fortress on the top of a mountain named Masada. It was at the edge of the Dead Sea. About 100 years later, the Romans captured Jerusalem. Nearly 1,000 Jewish people fled to the safety of the fortress in the desert. There they stayed for three years, fighting off attacks. When the Romans finally broke through, they found that the families had chosen to kill themselves rather than be taken as slaves. Today Masada is a symbol of courage and freedom.

Industry and agriculture

Until the 1970s, our major industry was **manufacturing**. We made processed food, textiles and clothing, furniture, fertilizers, and plastic and metal products. Over the past 20 years, Israel has moved into high-tech fields such as telecommunications, **agrotechnology**, medical electronics, and computer hardware and software. We are world leaders in the business of diamond cutting and polishing.

Tourism is also very important to our economy. Every year, thousands of people from around the world come to visit our archaeological and religious sites. They also enjoy our wonderful climate and beaches.

Using **drip irrigation**, farmers have managed to turn much of our barren desert into fertile land. Cotton, and fruit and vegetables such as avocados, melons, cucumbers, tomatoes, strawberries and citrus are all grown here. Flowers such as roses and carnations are grown to sell to other countries. Some farmers keep cows and poultry.

A salt factory near Sedom processes salt from the Dead Sea.

Palestinian boys harvesting zucchini. We export fruit and vegetables all over the world.

Half of our food is grown on special farming communities called kibbutzim. The people who live and work here share everything. Instead of wages, they receive food, education and a place to live. On another type of farm, called *moshav*, families are more independent of each other. They do not share everything.

Water sprinklers have been used for many years to irrigate our dry fields. But they can be wasteful. Much of the water sprays into the air and dries up before it reaches the roots of the plant. The drip system of watering is much more efficient. Long plastic tubes with holes in them allow water to drip directly onto the plants.

Transportation

In a small country like ours, the towns are close together. Cars, buses and trucks are the main forms of transportation. Our road network has been expanded in recent years. It now includes nearly 16,000 kilometers (10,000 miles) of highways. Even distant communities can now be reached by car.

The Egged bus system is owned by its drivers. It provides a cheap national transportation network.

Passenger trains run between Jerusalem, Tel Aviv, Haifa and Nahariya. Freight trains travel further south to the port of Ashdod, the cities of Ashkelon and Be'er Sheva, and the mines near Dimona. Fast trains work together with buses in the Tel Aviv and Haifa areas. They help free up crowded roads. Many of our old-fashioned trains are now being replaced by modern air-conditioned ones.

Cars, buses and taxis are our main forms of transportation. Communal taxis, called sherut, *have six doors and can take up to seven passengers.*

There are three deep-water harbors at Haifa, Eilat and Ashdod. They are used for international shipping. Haifa is one of the largest container ports on the Mediterranean Sea. It is also a busy passenger terminal. Ben-Gurion International Airport, near Tel Aviv, is our main air terminal.

Our national airline is El Al. It is named after a biblical phrase meaning 'on high'.

History and government

The State of Israel was only created in 1948, but our people have a long history. Nearly 4,000 years ago, a man named Abraham led a tribe of **nomadic people** across the desert from Mesopotamia (now Iraq) to the land of Canaan (the country now known as Israel). There are many stories about Abraham in the Bible. The Jewish people call him the 'father of our nation'.

Many years later, there was a famine. Abraham's grandson Jacob took his 12 sons and their families to Egypt, to find food. The Egyptians treated them as slaves, but they were later freed by Moses. According to the Bible, Moses convinced the people to worship God and follow special laws, called the Ten Commandments. Around 1250 BC, the 12 tribes returned to Canaan. Over the years, the area was conquered many times by different countries. The Romans called the area Palestine. During their rule, many Jews were driven out of Palestine. This was called the **Diaspora** or 'scattering'. Over the following centuries, Jews prayed that they would be able to return to their country one day.

*The remains of a Roman theater at Beit She'an, in the Lower Galilee region. Palestine became part of the **Roman Empire** in 63 BC.*

Excavations in the Old City of Jerusalem show the place where Jesus is said to have cured a paraplegic. This is written about in the Bible.

Around AD 600, Arabs occupied the area. Many Palestinians became Muslims. From the late 1800s, Jews from countries around Europe began to settle in Palestine. At that stage the country was ruled by Turkey. A group of Jews known as Zionists wanted Palestine to become a state where only Jews could live. The Arabs who were already living there fought against this plan.

In 1947, the United Nations voted to split Palestine into separate Jewish and Arab states. The Arabs opposed this idea, so Israel decided to declare itself an independent state in May 1948. Troops from six Arab countries invaded Israel and war raged for over a year. Since then, fighting between the Israelis and the Arabs over land has continued on and off.

Today Israel has a parliamentary democracy, which means people are able to vote for the political parties they want to represent them. Members of parliament are voted in every four years.

Fact file

Official name State of Israel	**Population** 5,850,000	**Land area** 20,770 square kilometers (8,000 square miles)
Government parliamentary democracy	**Languages** Hebrew (official), Arabic, English	**Religions** Judaism, Islam, Christianity
Currency New Israeli shekel (NIS) I new Israeli shekel = 100 new agorot	**Capital city** Jerusalem	**Major cities** Tel Aviv–Jaffa, Haifa, Be'er Sheva, Eilat
	Climate hot, dry summers and mild winters	
Major river Jordan	**Length of coastline** 273 kilometers (170 miles)	**Highest mountain** Mount Meron 1,208 meters (3,960 feet)
Main farm products citrus, vegetables, cotton, beef, poultry, dairy products	**Main industries** food processing, diamond cutting and polishing, clothing, chemicals, metal products, electronics, tourism	**Natural resources** copper, phosphates, bromide, potash, clay, sand, asphalt, natural gas, crude oil

Glossary

agrotechnology	better methods of growing crops
amphitheaters	outdoor stages used for plays and concerts. Their design allows people sitting at the back to hear what is happening on the stage
archaeological	refers to cultures of the past
Diaspora	when Jewish people were forced out of Israel and scattered all over the world
double-glazed	windows that have an extra layer of glass to help reduce noise from outside
drip irrigation	a system of providing water for fields using a series of pipes from which water drips onto plants
manufacturing	the making of goods in factories
matza	flat bread made without yeast, eaten during the Passover festival
melting pot	a place where large numbers of people from different cultures are mixed together
military service	a period of time which every Israeli must spend training with the armed forces
nomadic people	people who move around in search of food, instead of living in one place
prophet	a teacher or leader who claims to speak to God or Allah
renovated	refers to a house that has been changed to improve it
Roman Empire	refers to the countries that were ruled by Rome from 27 BC to AD 284
Sabbath	the weekly day of rest. Jewish people hold their Sabbath on Saturdays
sculpture	a work of art made by carving or shaping materials such as stone or wood
Zionism	a belief that there is a Jewish homeland in the Middle Eastern area where the Israelites originally lived. 'Zion' is another name for Jerusalem

Index